# 7 Questions Every Young Leader Must Answer

## By

## Randy D. Williams

*Ovation Publishing Group*

Printed in the United States of America

Published By:

Ovation Publishing Group

Portsmouth, Virginia

ISBN-10:  0615810578

ISBN-13: 978-0615810577

Library of Congress Cataloging-in-Publication Data


Williams, Randy D.

7 Questions Every Young Leader Must Answer

# Table of Contents

*Connect with Randy*

# Chapter 1
# Who Are You?

"Don't be known for what you present; be known for what you represent."

*Randy D. Williams*

"Who are you?" This is the most difficult question for many of us to answer. When asked this question, our natural inclination is to answer with our name. Sure, that's what we are called but who we are is much more involved than that. Names don't *define* who we are. They simply serve as words that spark a thought or memory when people hear them.

For example, what comes to mind when you hear LeBron James or Halle Berry? How about Adolf Hitler or Osama Bin Laden? Or maybe even Barack Obama or Donald Trump? I'm sure as you read each name you thought about the things that make each individual famous or infamous. You remembered a significant character trait about each individual, and you no doubt have an opinion about that person. You probably also thought about something they did very well or very badly. All of the things you thought of when hearing those names are the things that truly define who those people are.

Don't become known only by your name. Be known for what you represent. "Who are you?" This question requires a response filled with information about your character and values. Don't feel bad if you can't answer the question right away. It takes time to discover exactly what you stand for. We are very complex people whose desires, dreams and visions change frequently, but eventually we find something that makes our heart flutter. That's the thing that creates such a passion in us that we know we were born to do it. As you read this book, the wheels of your imagination will begin to turn. This road of self-discovery will lead you right to the thing that really makes you come alive. The first step to self-discovery is truly defining who you are.

*An Eagle Among Chickens*

Imagine an eagle hatched in a chicken coup. The chicks and the eagle eat, sleep and play together, but soon the young chicks notice that the eagle's feathers aren't yellow like theirs. Furthermore, when the young birds begin to grow, the chicks notice that the eagle is a lot bigger than the other birds. Because the eagle is bigger, he also eats a lot more than his "brothers and sisters." Despite his differences, the mother chicken raises the eagle as her own and doesn't treat him any differently.

Let's fast forward a few years. The eagle is all grown up, but he can't fly. I know what you're saying; eagles are known for their superb flying ability, right? Of course they are, but this eagle has spent his entire life pecking around on the farm and eating the seeds being thrown at him. Since he's been hanging out with chickens, he never had the opportunity to meet another eagle who would teach him to soar high above the clouds like other eagles. He lives his life on the ground, never experiencing the wind in his massive wings and never knowing who he is truly meant to be. The chicken coup doesn't transform the eagle into a chicken, but it does prevent him from discovering his true potential.

Do you know anyone who lives a life similar to that of the eagle? Most of us know someone who is living life as someone they really aren't meant to be. They haven't realized that they are really eagles! They don't know that they are some of the most skilled hunters in the animal kingdom. They don't even know that they have unparalleled vision and fearlessness. They don't know how high they can actually soar.

Most people can't define who they are because they don't understand who they aren't. If the eagle knew that he was *not* a chicken, his life would be dramatically different. Only by realizing what he is *not* can he begin to discover what he truly is. There are two simple truths that you should understand.

1. You are not defined by what you have.

2. You are not defined by who others say you are.

The goal of this book is to challenge you to ask yourself the tough questions that will help you discover who you are and how high you were really meant to soar.

*Can you see me?*

Avoiding the temptation to define ourselves by what we have is difficult. Society has an addiction to outward displays of wealth and power. We make lightning-quick assumptions about people we meet based on the most superficial characteristics. For example, if I asked you what kind of car the richest man in the world drives, what would come to mind? Most people would assume that he drives a $300,000, high-powered, exotic car. You probably picture a bright-colored automobile that catches the eye of everyone on the highway. On the contrary, the richest man in the world probably doesn't drive much, but the second richest man in the world (Warren Buffett at the time of this writing) drives a $40,000 Cadillac! This fact catches most people by surprise because they buy into the stereotypes of how wealthy individuals spend their money. They assume that because those people have more money, they automatically buy the most expensive, high-end, exclusive possessions, but that is not always the case. I used this illustration to stress how important it is to not let these stereotypes create a distorted view of life for you. Oftentimes, the glamorous life that we see portrayed in the media is not reality.

Most people emulate the lifestyles of the rich and famous celebrities plastered on television and the internet. They aspire to dress like the rich and famous and drive the cars the celebrities drive. They buy into this lifestyle not knowing that most of it is a façade.

When a woman buys a designer handbag, she is buying more than just a device to carry her personal items. She is buying a feeling. She wants the feeling of knowing that she has one of the most sought after handbags available. She is also buying the adoration of her peers. She can hardly wait to carry the bag in public so that a random stranger can compliment her on it.

I challenge you to think a little differently. No, I'm not saying that you shouldn't own nice things, but I am suggesting that you make sure these things don't own you. Let your personal desires influence your purchasing decisions. Don't be swayed by the desires of others. Be aware of the fact that life is far more important than any material possession. Make important things like love, service and achievement your top priorities.

*Define Yourself*

It is important to formulate your own definition of who you are.  As we answer the other six questions in this book, that definition will become clearer. Oftentimes, we let the opinions of others prevent us from becoming who we are meant to be. For example, did you or anyone you know dream of becoming a professional athlete?  I did. I used to spend hours and hours practicing basketball in my backyard.  I dreamt of hearing the crowds roar as I scored the winning shot. I could also imagine the looks of approval that the fans would give me. I imagined high-five's from the fans as I walked down the corridor before and after each game. Playing basketball for me was not all about a love for the sport; it was about the respect and adoration that I could receive from others. Anytime we are motivated by validation from others, we put ourselves in a dangerous place. It causes us to become dependent on things outside of ourselves to be happy. No one but *you* should have the power to control your feelings and emotions.

Have you ever had to fight a family member or friend over the remote control? Maybe there was a show that you wanted to watch, but the other person wanted to watch something different. Usually, the person who holds the remote control has the most power to determine which channel the television lands on.  If you want to watch the sports channel and your friend wants to watch a music video, who is right? I challenge you to hold the remote control for your life and determine the channel your life lands on.

## Chapter Reflections

1. Define yourself in one sentence.

_____

_____

_____

_____

2. List the three most valuable things that you possess.

_____

_____

_____

_____

3. List the three most valuable qualities you possess.

_____

_____

_____

_____

4. Compare your list of most valuable things to your list of most valuable qualities. Which ones are more important? Why?

_____

_____

_____

_____

# Chapter 2

## Who Are Your Friends?

"Show me your friends, and I'll show you your future."

*Randy D. Williams*

---

Have you ever been betrayed by someone you considered a friend? Most of us have. Your initial thought is one of shock and amazement that a person so close to you could betray you in such a manner. Pretty soon your feelings of shock and amazement are replaced by feelings of anger. You begin to think of ways to defend yourself and ways to pay them back for the harm that they have caused you. After you have passed the anger phase, sadness sets in as you think of how disappointed you are to have lost someone that was close to you.

The process of gaining and losing a friend can be quite a rollercoaster. You can experience many different emotions one after the other, and the loss can leave you feeling more confused than ever. Unfortunately, your life will never be the same because you will second guess your future friendships. You will wonder if each new person that you meet will disappoint you like your former friend did.

As a young leader, it is critical to establish consistency in your environment. A big part of that is related to the people with whom you spend your time. Having the right inner circle is one of the secrets to success, and creating the right inner circle should never be rushed.

I remember taking a vocabulary test when I was in grade school. I had studied my flash cards all night, and I was sure that I was going to ace the test. I answered each question with confidence, and I was one of the first students to finish. I confidently waited for the papers to be graded so that I could take my A+ home and show it off to my family. When the teacher gave me the graded test, I noticed some red ink; I had gotten two questions wrong! I aggressively asked my teacher to explain this less-than-perfect score. She said, "You got those two questions mixed up." In my rush to finish the test, I had mistakenly answered one question with the correct answer for another. I had gotten the definitions confused.

Many of us are confused about the definition of a friend. I often hear others call someone a "friend" shortly after the first meeting. It's usually too soon. The word "friend" is something that we should take a bit more seriously. Instead of rushing into being friends with someone, we should evaluate whether or not that person adds value to our lives. Merriam Webster's dictionary defines a friend as "a person attached to another by feelings of affection or personal regard." The key word in that definition is "attached." When we become friends with another person, we become attached to him or her. In essence, that person becomes a part of us, and we become a part of that person. You may view a friend as just someone with whom you can have fun, but a true friendship is a much deeper attachment.

There are four primary characteristics your friends should have. Having friends with these traits will give you the greatest chance to live a successful life. I like to call these types of friends D.E.E.P.

Dependable

The first characteristic of a great friend is dependability. You want to know that you can count on that person in a time of need. Let's say you were stranded in the middle of nowhere and needed a ride home. Which one of your friends comes to mind? What if you were out of money and needed something to eat? Who would you call first? Your answers to those questions should help you determine if you have dependable friends. One of the biggest mistakes that we make when choosing friends is labeling them as dependable too soon.

Dependability is something that is proven over time. Friends earn the dependable title when they have shown time and time again that they will be there when needed. When we rush to put titles on people undeservedly, we set ourselves up for huge disappointments. Unfortunately, there is no shortcut when it comes to having dependable people around you. The greatest tool to determine a friend's dependability is time. It is through long-term interaction and observation that true friends are revealed.

Encouraging

A real friend is also very encouraging. You may have a goal of being a sought after violinist who travels the country playing in some of the world's most renowned venues. If you are serious about this goal, you know that you must practice playing your instrument many hours each week. There will be many times when your practice times will interfere with leisure activities. A true friend would not ask you to skip practice to hang out or tell you that what you're doing is dumb. A true friend will postpone leisure activities to include you and will only want to encourage you to strive to be the best that you can be.

There will be times when we will not feel like studying or practicing or reading. It is during these times that our friends should remind us that we can do it and that we are on our way to becoming great. They are like the coach of a rowing team. Even though the team members do all of the hard work, they need a coach to push them when their muscles get tight and they don't think that they can go any faster. The coach yells "row" every time the oar hits the water. It is this reminder and encouragement that keeps them going. Great friends do the same for us.

Exciting

Good friends are also exciting. You should be able to have fun with the people around you. Having common interests usually attracts us to one another. Most people who are good friends understand and appreciate how the other person behaves. Think about how many inside jokes you have with your current friends. Sharing a common bond and sense of humor usually brings people together. It is just as important to be able to enjoy extracurricular activities with others as it is to focus on becoming a good student. It is during these fun bonding moments that true and lasting friendships are solidified. Being able to balance your personal goals and your fun times is critically important.

Purposeful

Lastly, a friend should be purposeful. It amazes me how many of us spend time with people who have no sense of purpose in life. They have no goals or dreams and we risk picking up many of their bad habits. Do you know someone who is floating aimlessly through life? They spend most of their days discovering new ways to "kill time." Some of these people waste time by playing video games, watching television or chatting on social networks. No matter the method, people who waste time often finish the day in the same place they started it.

As a college student, I can remember going to the student union to play table tennis. I was not a very good player, but I enjoyed the game because it gave me the opportunity to relax after a long day of classes. It was a fun activity, but after a few months I began to notice a pattern. Each time I went into the student union, I saw the same people there! Even when I was just passing by, I would see them still there. I quickly determined that these students could not have been devoting much of their time to studying and reaching the goal that everyone on campus shared – graduation. My speculations were right. One-by-one these people dropped out of college. The ones that did not drop out simply repeated the same classes. I saw very few of these people during graduation because they somehow lost track of what was important.

Real friends live their lives with purpose. They manage their time and resources in a way that pushes them toward their goals and dreams. Associating yourself with people who feel the same way will help you stay on track toward reaching your goals.

Be sure to find friends that are D.E.E.P. (Dependable, Encouraging, Exciting and Purposeful). Using these four characteristics as a guide will help you to determine who your true friends are and also allow you to connect with those who can help you the most.

## Chapter Reflections

1.  After reading this chapter, how will you change your friend circle?   Why?

_____

_____

_____

_____

2.  List your D.E.E.P. friends.

_____

_____

_____

_____

3.  What are some ways that you can become a better friend to others?

_____

_____

_____

_____

# Chapter 3

# What Are Your Habits?

"Only habits separate amateurs from professionals."

*Randy D. Williams*

I saw a commercial at the time of this writing that made me think. The commercial featured a woman getting ready in the mirror. She applied makeup to her damaged skin, put a wig on her bald head and a scarf around her neck to cover a hole from throat surgery. The commercial was sponsored by the Surgeon General of the United States. The intent was to make the public aware of the dangers of smoking cigarettes. The commercial, along with several others that are very similar, feature people who have irreparably damaged their bodies through a lifetime of smoking. Nonsmokers see the commercial and say, "I'm never going to smoke cigarettes. That's a no brainer," but each day people continue to smoke with knowledge of the risks, which include cancer, lung disease and heart disease. There has to be only one reason why someone would continue to smoke despite the risk factors. They smoke because it is a habit. Not surprisingly, most smokers that I have spoken with genuinely want to quit smoking, and they would if they believed that it was possible for them. However, the habit has become such a part of their way of living that many no longer try to stop.

*The Power of Habits*

Have you ever flown on a plane? If so, you probably noticed and greeted the pilot as you boarded the aircraft. If you have had the opportunity to look inside of the pilot's cockpit, you know that there are hundreds of buttons, knobs, lights and levers designed to make sure the aircraft arrives at its destination safely. What you probably don't know is that for the majority of the flight the plane is actually flying itself. There is something called autopilot that makes the flight safer and the jobs of today's pilots so much easier. Autopilot minimizes the errors that can be made by pilots due to various conditions. Once the coordinates are entered into the computers onboard the plane, it is pretty easy for the plane to get to its destination.

Our personal habits are much like the autopilot feature used on most airplanes. They allow us to automatically arrive at a predetermined destination in life. For some of us, that destination could be a warm, tropical Caribbean paradise, but for others it could be a lonely, cold and dark Siberian cave. The good news is that we all have an opportunity to arrive at the destination of our choice. We can do this by creating the right habits.

*Why We Need Habits*

Much like autopilot, our good habits allow us to minimize the mistakes that we will make on our journey to reach success. For example, if I develop the habit of eating fresh fruits and vegetables and other foods that are packed with nutrients, then it will be a lot easier to reach my goal of being healthier and living longer. However, if I develop the habit of eating greasy, high-fat, high-calorie foods with little nutritional value, then I will actually move in the opposite direction of my goals. So, we need habits to keep us on track for achieving success in our lives. Unfortunately, most people use habits in a way that pushes them further away from what they want.

Athletes use the power of habits all of the time. Just take a look at your favorite sport, and you will notice

many of the benefits of using habits to your advantage. Soccer players must control a ball using only their feet while running full speed. Basketball players must time their jumps perfectly to block a defender's shot. Baseball players must determine in milliseconds if it is ok to swing at the pitch being thrown. Football players must ward off a defender, catch the ball and keep their feet in bounds in the blink of an eye.

No matter the sport, the players' bodies must react faster than their minds can actually think. Decisions are made so quickly that every reaction of the athletes' bodies must be involuntary, and that high level of play can only occur when the athletes have developed habits that will allow them to react without having to think about what to do next. We can see these types of results in our personal lives as well. With the right habits, we too can perform at a very high level and become professionals in our chosen fields and areas of interest.

Habits can also help us avoid distractions. I have a friend who goes to the gym six days a week. He is so passionate about fitness that very few things can derail his workout routine. There have been times when his friends have invited him to other places, but he respectfully declines if it interferes with his gym schedule. When he plans out-of-town vacations, he selects a hotel with a gym that meets his workout needs. Even though he may want to deviate from his normal routine, his habits keep him on track for achieving his goals.

*HOP = Habits On Purpose*

Although most people won't admit it, habits are not formed overnight. They are formed by doing something so much that it becomes second nature. Studies have shown that it takes approximately 21 days of repetitive action to establish a habit. So, think about the implications of the deliberate habit-forming process for those of us seeking success. Those who infuse their lives with deliberate processes practice what I call the HOP method. HOP is an acronym for Habits On Purpose. Instead of allowing the habits to form without your knowledge, perform your new habit for at least 21 days. Armed with the knowledge that habits don't just happen, we can now take control of our actions. We can make the process of developing new habits intentional.

So what new habits would you like to create? Think about some current habits that are limiting your productivity. For example, most people have the habit of coming home, flopping down on the couch and turning on the television. Think about how different your life would be if you changed that habit. Instead of coming home and watching television, immediately begin doing something more productive when you get home. If your goal is to be an honor student, you should come home and study first. For others who may play an instrument, try practicing for one hour before doing anything else. If you want a new job, why not come home and begin completing your application first? Apply the HOP method and watch your life change.

Some people are intimidated by the HOP method. They say things like, "I've been doing it this way too long" or my favorite, "That's just the way I am." This book was written to show you that no matter what you have believed in the past, it is possible to create new ways of thinking. Your new thinking will lead to new behavior. As you embark on this journey, it's important to take small steps. Doing so will help you avoid intimating thoughts. Many people start their success journey by setting life-changing goals, but when they don't achieve them fast enough they become discouraged. It is important to remember that changing your habits is a step-by-step process that begins slowly.

When I was a preteen, I wanted to grow taller. Even though I had no control over it, I would measure myself everyday against my bedroom wall. I knew I was going to hit a growth spurt, but I just did not know *when* it would happen. I was discouraged when weeks went by with no measurable (or minimal) progress. I eventually stopped measuring my height and put the goal behind me. About a year later, I remembered that I was supposed to be checking back periodically, and I had grown two inches! My body continued to grow automatically even though I wasn't able to see results as quickly as I wanted. Our habits are the same way. When we make our behavior automatic, a positive outcome is guaranteed. Sometimes we can't see the immediate results we want, but we should not get discouraged. Just remember that sometimes success happens slowly.

## Chapter Reflections

1. What are some bad habits you need to break now?

_____

_____

_____

_____

2. What are some new habits that you would like to create?

_____

_____

_____

_____

3. What steps will you take to create the new habits?

_____

_____

_____

_____

# Chapter 4
## Who Is Influencing You?

"Influence is the vehicle through which ideas are transferred."

*Randy D. Williams*

*Who is Influencing You?*

When I was younger, I remember planting a seed in a red plastic cup for a school project. Each person in the class was given soil and a seed. We labeled the cups with our names and waited patiently for the seeds to grow into flowers. Each day when we returned to the classroom, I rushed over to the cup with my name on it to check the progress. After a couple of weeks, the seeds began to sprout, and we could see the plant grow every day. Soon, we were allowed to take the plants home and care for them ourselves. I placed my plant in the window sill in our kitchen, but after a few days I noticed something strange; my plant was leaning towards the window. To fix this, I turned the plant around but after a few days the plant still leaned towards the window. The next day I rushed up to my teacher and asked, "Why

does my plant lean to one side?" She told me it was because of the plant's desire to be near the sunlight.

I think our lives mirror that of the plant that I had in grade school. Whether we know it or not, we lean towards those things that have the greatest influence on us. Instead of sunlight, we tend to lean towards (act and think like) the media, philosophies and people that are closest to us. It is our responsibility as leaders to monitor and control the things that we allow into our lives.

*Media*

As a leader, you must not underestimate the impact of media on your growth and development. Many years ago, the most revolutionary media available to us was the radio. It was quite an experience to sit next to the radio a few nights per week and listen to your favorite show. Soon after radio became popular, businesses began to market their products to the people listening to the radio shows. The way we consume media has never been the same. Since then, the abundance and availability of media has skyrocketed. Today, there is a marketing message or news story at every turn. Instead of being scarce, information is now at our fingertips whenever we want it. If you attempted to count the number of marketing messages that you consume every day, I'm sure you would lose count.

The first thing that most of us do in the morning after we wake up is grab our cell phones or turn on our televisions. These two devices alone are filled with more marketing messages than we can stomach. On your way to work or school, you will see hundreds of advertisements in the form of billboards and car signage and hear hundreds more on the radio. When you arrive to your destination, you no doubt will see clothing with logos intended to sway your opinion of that particular brand and influence you to purchase their products. McDonald's, for example, still spends on average over $2 billion each year on its advertising to ensure that it remains one of the number one fast food chains. If companies are willing to spend that type of money to get your attention, then we should pay closer attention to how it directly affects us.

*Using Media to Your Advantage*

I grew up in a very small town, so there were many things to which I was not exposed. Furthermore, when I was growing up it was very difficult for me to find positive role models. Since I had no one to look up to, I had to look to other places to find these role models. One way to develop yourself as a leader is to use media to find positive examples of success. Since I wanted to be an entrepreneur, I looked for TV shows and movies that gave me a glimpse into the lifestyle I wanted. In this way, I used media to my advantage instead of letting it negatively affect me.

Other forms of media include books, magazines, video and audio. Typically, we use these forms of media for entertainment purposes only, but I'd like to challenge you to use them for personal growth. You can help your future immensely by reading books like this one. Read books that challenge you to think and act differently. Read one book per month that is related to an area the interests you. If you are a person who is on-the-go, try audio books that you can listen to in your car or on your mp3 player. Instead of reading a celebrity gossip magazine, try reading a magazine related to a field that you would like to go into. This will give you a wealth of information in your field and give you a head start on your competition. Remember, the more time you devote to something, the more expertise you develop in it.

*Don't Follow the Crowd*

I remember sitting in my college class waiting on my teacher to arrive. The class started at 11:00, and at 11:10 our teacher had not arrived. Pretty soon, we all started to look around at each other as we wondered if our professor would arrive. Since I was only a freshman, I had no idea what to do in these types of situations. As I pondered what to do next, another student yelled out, "Man I'm leaving!" As he gathered his things and walked out of the door, his friends followed. After another couple of minutes passed, a few more students left the class, assuming that the teacher was not coming. By 11:14, about 90 percent of the students had left, and only a couple of us remained. As a rule, the university required us to wait at least 15 minutes for our professor to arrive. As soon as the clock struck 11:15, our professor came walking through the door almost out of breath and exclaimed, "Where is everybody?" The three of us that were still there laughed and explained that the rest of the class thought she was a no-show. Instead of getting angry she said, "Well this is your lucky day. Take out a sheet of paper because we are about to have a pop quiz!" We all moaned in anguish as we pulled out our sheets of paper. Someone mumbled, "I knew I should've left." The professor continued, "This quiz has only one question so it won't take very long.

Please answer the following question: What day of the week is it?" We all laughed and wrote "Thursday" on our paper. That was the easiest "A" that I had ever received.

As a leader, you must remember that doing the right thing is often the opposite of what the crowd is doing. In this case, if I had left the classroom I would have damaged my grade and risked failing the class. Instead, I was rewarded for doing the right thing even though it was unpopular.

## Following is Easy

It is very easy to follow the crowd instead of having the courage to stand on your own. Following the crowd is easy because you don't have to think. When you are simply a follower, you let others think for you. I'd like to challenge you to start making your own decisions instead of blindly following the crowd or doing something simply because it is popular. Before you do anything, always ask yourself, "Why?" Unfortunately, most people don't ask themselves this question because it forces them to think critically. When we think critically, we transition from passive thinking to active thinking, and this active thinking requires work, focus and intelligence. When my professor showed up late for class, it would have been easy to follow my classmates and leave the class before the instructor arrived. It was much harder to remain in my seat after most of my classmates had left. As I watched them leave, I imagined what they might think of me. Would they call me a nerd or a teacher's pet? No matter what they may have called me, I knew I had an obligation to do what was right.

*Everyday Influence*

Many times we are being influenced even though we are not aware of it. When celebrities start wearing a particular brand of clothing, you're likely to see the trend spread. Before you know it, everyone is wearing what the celebrities wear. This is an example of influence. Those who like the celebrity's style, talent and persona will quickly determine that his or her clothing choice is a good one and mimic it. Even during presidential elections, the public's opinion was swayed by highlighting the accomplishments of one candidate and highlighting the failures of another. Many times you will hear someone say, "I don't like Candidate X," but if you were to ask them why it would be extremely hard for them to distinguish one candidate's platform from another. Oftentimes, our opinions of others are influenced by second-hand information with very little investigation of our own.

*Choose to Be a Leader*

You must choose to be a leader at school, at work and in your community. Instead of following what's popular, use your leadership skills to influence those around you. Instead of influencing those around you to do something cool, influence them to make difference in the world. Is there a community service project that you feel very strongly about? If so, you can encourage others to get involved in your cause. Maybe there is a city park for kids that needs to be cleaned up. A friend of mine gathers a group of his peers and feeds the homeless twice a year. Another person I know collects winter coats for needy families. If you don't have an idea of your own, join an

organization in your area that is making a difference.
I have volunteered my time, energy and money to
help build houses for those in need, feed the homeless
and deliver Christmas toys to children whose parents
weren't able to buy gifts. These experiences gave me a
heart for service, and I now know that true leadership
is about being able to serve others.

## Chapter Reflections

1. Who is the most influential person in your life right now?

_____
_____
_____
_____

2. Name some celebrities that have influenced the way you think.

_____
_____
_____
_____

3. Describe a time when following the crowd was a bad idea.

_____
_____
_____
_____

# Chapter 5

# Who Are Your Mentors?

"Having a mentor is like taking an open book test. The answers are right in front of you, but you still have to find them yourself."

*Randy D. Williams*

A mentor provides insight and advice to those who are looking to rapidly expand their knowledge. Usually, a mentor is an older, more experienced person who has specialized knowledge in a field or area of life that you wish to learn more about. For example, a coach is like a mentor to those who play sports. The coach provides guidance and helps athletes get better at the game. Furthermore, a coach helps the players to create a strategy that will allow them to win the game. Your mentor can help you win the game of life. Coaches and mentors draw up a game plan for us, and it's our job to execute the plays. In the heat of battle we can get overwhelmed because it seems that we are losing the game and have no chance of success. The one common denominator of all great teams is that they have a coach that players can turn to when things become too difficult for them

to handle on their own.

I remember when I was a manager for my high school

basketball team. During my term as manager, our

high school team won one of three consecutive state

championships. Being able to see what went into

making the team successful gave me a lot of insight

into what it requires to be a champion. On the night

of the championship game, emotions were very high.

Because the team was so good, fans always packed

the venue and had become accustomed to watching a

winning game. Some of the fans were even arrogant.

The basketball team, on the other hand, was anything

but arrogant. Even though they played at a very high

level, they always remained level-headed. It was

amazing to see them on the court because they

operated like a well-oiled machine, even in high-pressure situations. Our team was known for its endurance and was always able to play at full pace no matter how tough the competition. They made winning games look very easy, but I knew what their real secret was; the coach made every player on the team better.

During practice, the team ran plays until those plays became second nature to them. If someone made the wrong move or made a bad decision, the coach would offer feedback to correct the play. The players shot at least 100 free throws during each practice, so they very rarely missed free throws during the game. The biggest key to their success was their conditioning. The coach made them run wind sprints at the end of each practice; even though they hated them, the exercise gave them the endurance to become a championship team.

Our mentors may require us to do things that we don't really like, but those things make us better players. Many of our basketball players went on to play college basketball at Division-I schools and even played professionally.

*Qualities of a Good Mentor*

Great mentors are like parents because they teach us how to live healthy and productive lives. The guidance that they offer is invaluable, and it often pushes us toward our success. Conversely, not having a good mentor may slow your ability to be successful. It is important to identify the qualities that make a great mentor. Once you have identified the right qualities, you will know how to select a great mentor. There are two main qualities that a great mentor possesses, willingness and expertise.

There are many successful people that we would like to emulate. We may see that they have accomplished many of the things that we desire to accomplish, and we may begin to think that they could be a great mentor. Many of these people simply are not willing to become a mentor to you. Some people have time constraints that prevent them from giving you the attention that you need to grow and develop, so they decline the opportunity to assist you. Some may already have mentees and have very little time for you. Still, others may have the time and availability yet they simply do not have the passion to mentor others.

Willingness is such an important quality because your ideal mentor will be someone who is passionate about making others successful. They must have a desire to teach others the lessons that they have learned along the way, and many people simply aren't interested in that. A great mentor that has a burning desire to accelerate your success is the best type of person to have guiding you.

Other potential mentors may have the time and willingness, but they fail to have the expertise that you need. I remember seeing an ad posted on my college bulletin board that said "FREE TUTORING." Since I was having a tough time with college algebra and could not afford to pay for tutoring, I decided to attend a session to see if it would help. I arrived at the location and noticed a few students being helped by some tutors. A fellow student approached me and asked if I needed some help. I was so excited to have the opportunity to have someone teach me a subject that was so difficult to me. I pulled out my math book and homework and begin to ask how he could help me. In the middle of my sentence, he cut me off and pointed to the sign on the wall that said "Science Tutoring." I had reached a tutor, but unfortunately his expertise was in another area and he couldn't help me.

This story illustrates how important it is to find the right mentor for you. When I needed help with college algebra, an expert in the field of math would have been able to add tremendous value to my situation and help me with my homework; however, the science tutor was not able to help me. Even though the tutor was passionate, he needed to have some expertise in the field that I needed help with in order to make me successful. A true mentor will provide the specific tools and knowledge needed to make you successful.

*Finding a Mentor*

There are many different ways to find a mentor that will help you along your road to success. Most often a mentor will not come and find you; you will have to find a mentor. Some great mentors don't even know you exist, but that doesn't mean that they aren't willing to help you. For some, the process of finding a mentor happens very quickly, but for others it takes a while. There is no one-size-fits-all way to select and convince the right person to mentor you, but there are some things that you can do to put yourself in the best possible position.

*Determine What You Need*

One of the first things you can do is create a list of the things that you would like your mentor to help you with. Do you need someone to help motivate you? Do you need someone to give you career advice? Do you want someone who will show you techniques for doing something better? Whatever your needs are, remember to write them down and compare them to the potential mentors to see which mentor is the best match for you.

*What You Have to Offer*

In addition to writing down what you need from a mentor, also take the time to write down the things that you will provide as a mentee. What qualities do you bring to the table? What things are you good at? Think about how you can help your mentor do a better job at what he or she does. During your research process, find a mentor that you can help in some way. Remember, your relationship with a mentor is not one-sided; you must add value to the relationship as well.

*Researching a Mentor*

The internet is a great research tool. You can use it to find and research the people who may make great mentors for you. You can use the internet to find their experience in the field, organizations they are affiliated with, personality traits, political and religious views, favorite sports teams and much more. All of these elements will help you determine if you are choosing a person with whom you will be able to get along. By finding out important information about your potential mentor in advance, you can weed out those with whom you don't have much in common. All of this information will help you streamline your list of potential mentors.

*Contacting a Mentor*

The last and most important step is to actually contact the potential mentors. You can contact them by phone or email or approach them face-to-face. The key here is to find a contact method that is most effective and most convenient for your potential mentor. Remember, don't get discouraged if you don't get a response to your first few attempts. Oftentimes, potential mentors are very busy, and it may take a while to make initial contact, so don't take it personally. Furthermore, many mentors admire persistence and enjoy mentoring people who don't give up quickly, so your persistence may be a good thing.  On the other hand, make sure you know when to move on. Don't become a pest to someone who has repeatedly told you that he or she is not interested. Just respect their wishes and move on because there are many other well-qualified people who can assist you.

Versatility is the key to being a good mentee. Be willing to put forth extra effort to establish the mentor/mentee relationship. Try to make it as easy as possible for your mentor to assist you with your goals. A great mentee is not only inspired *by* his or her mentor, but a great mentee inspires his or her mentor as well. You should inspire your mentor to become better at what he or she does.

Chapter Reflections

1. List five potential mentors.

_____

_____

_____

_____

_____

2. In what areas of expertise would you like your mentor to be knowledgeable?

_____

_____

_____

_____

_____

3. List five things you will bring to the mentor/mentee relationship.

_____

_____

_____

_____

_____

_____

# Chapter 6

# How Good Is Your Work Ethic?

"Work ethic separates the average from the exceptional."

*Randy D. Williams*

*Lazy Generation?*

One of the biggest criticisms that I heard growing up was that my generation was lazy and that we didn't want to work for anything. Of course, I brushed it off like most people my age, but it never really made sense until I got older. I realized that most of the modern luxuries that we take for granted were not available or even thought of when our parents and grandparents were young. Decades ago, there was no indoor plumbing, air travel, central heat and air, mobile phones and modern medicine. My parents didn't even have the internet. Imagine that! Over time, I realized that it wasn't that the younger generation couldn't work as hard. It was that they didn't *have* to. My generation is just as smart, talented and resourceful as past generations. It's just that we have never had to experience what our parents experienced. Many would view this as a handicap, but I view it as an opportunity. We now have an opportunity to learn the principles of hard work that made our parents successful, and apply them to a new set of rules in an economy with more powerful tools and opportunities. In essence, younger generations should always surpass previous ones because they are able to extract the best things from the past and make those things even better.

*Chores*

One of my least favorite tasks growing up was raking leaves. I absolutely hated it. I grew up in Southwest Georgia, and there were two things that we had a surplus of - trees and heat. Almost every yard had multiple trees with leaves that would fall to the ground and eventually need to be raked.

Unfortunately, the weather remained hot and humid for the majority of the year. There were a few things that made raking leaves my most-hated chore. The heat was definitely one of the top reasons. Raking took a few hours to complete, and by the time I finished I would be drenched in sweat and drained from the sun beaming down on me. I also hated this chore because each time I raked I would develop a blister between my index finger and my thumb because of the repetitive motion of the rake. The time-consuming nature of the task also made raking my least favorite chore. As a young child who valued his free time, I knew that having to rake meant that I could kiss my playtime goodbye for that day. Sometimes, my friends would stop by and ask me to play, but I had to decline their offer and keep raking until the entire yard was finished. There are a few principles that I learned from raking leaves as a kid that can help you achieve your goals faster.

*One Step at a Time*

When I looked out at the size of our backyard, I quickly became discouraged. It's easy to spend hours, days, weeks and years focusing on the size of the massive task ahead of you. Because of this habit, many people continue to procrastinate and make very little progress toward their goals. One thing that helps me is focusing on making just a little progress at a time. It's easy to become overwhelmed when you look at how much work is required to complete the entire task. When raking leaves, I focused on making several small piles of leaves first. Soon, I would begin to see that the end was near. You can do this with any task that is ahead of you. If it's homework, focus on doing the first question. If it's exercise focus on completing the first set, and if it's creating a work of art focus on the first brush stroke.

*Take Action*

A common trait of successful people is that they take action consistently. Very rarely do they have to be prodded or coerced into making a move. They have learned that taking action may create short-term pain, but it eliminates long-term regrets. I knew that I could have tried to argue with my grandmother and make excuses about why it wasn't fair that I had to rake the yard, but I quickly learned that this would only prolong the process, and eventually I would have to do it anyway. Our lives are the same. We can possibly delay the task ahead of us, but if we fail to take action now, the future consequences can be severe. Another common misconception that I had about hard work was that I had to *feel* like doing it. Truth be told, most of the action that is needed for success does not feel good. I saw boxing champion Manny Pacquiao do 1,000 crunches as a part of his workout routine. I'm sure that doing 1,000 crunches hurts (and I never plan on finding out if that's the case), but that's the pain we must often endure if we intend to be successful. Champions take action and work hard, even if it hurts.

*Five Benefits of Hard Work*

Achieve goals faster

When you consistently work hard, you will notice that you complete more tasks than those around you. Once the habit is created, tasks will become easier and easier. You will soon notice that people complain about doing things that require very little effort. Work ethic truly separates the average from the exceptional.

Improved reputation

Hard workers also become recognized by their peers for their efforts. Others will begin to look up to you because of your achievements, and you will be recognized as a leader. Being recognized as a leader creates even more new opportunities for you.

Less guilt

Those who fail to achieve goals due to laziness are forced to live with the guilt of not giving it their all. They are tormented each day with thoughts of *What if?* Oftentimes, they begin to think of themselves as underachievers, and in turn, they become even more unproductive. When you work hard consistently, you have confidence in knowing that you put forth the best effort possible.

Less Stress

Stress is caused when your current state of being is not your desired state of being. It dramatically decreases the quality of life that you live, both mentally and physically. Those who are stressed are less likely to operate at a high level. Fortunately, most of this stress is preventable. By simply accomplishing tasks as they present themselves, you avoid letting multiple tasks weigh you down. Those who work hard and finish tasks quickly are able to focus on fewer things and live a less stressful life.

*Happiness*

Ultimately, all leaders are seeking one thing – happiness. There are many paths to happiness, but the end result is a common one among leaders. Those who are more productive live happier lives because they are consistently realizing their dreams coming true. Each day puts them closer to their goals and the life that they've always wanted.

Great leaders not only possess superior work ethic, but they are able to motivate others to work just as hard as they do. It is important to set the example as the leader in your school, workplace and community. Being a leader is not always easy, but it is always worth it.

## Chapter Reflections

1.  What are some areas that you know you could work harder in?

    _____
    _____
    _____
    _____

2.  How would improving your work ethic help you become successful?

    _____
    _____
    _____
    _____

3.  List five people whose work ethic you admire. Why?

    _____
    _____
    _____
    _____

# Chapter 7

## What are you passionate about?

"The fastest way to discover your passions is to look for ways to serve others."

*Randy D. Williams*

_____

One of the biggest road blocks most people face on their path to success is their inability to discover what they are truly passionate about. Unfortunately, we face pressure and scrutiny from many outside influences such as parents, peers and media on a daily basis. These outside influences can change our opinions about what we want to do with our lives and which paths we take on the road to success. It is important to find out what your passions are because you will never live a life that is truly satisfying until you do so. Many who fail to discover their passions will battle feelings of inadequacy and emptiness. Each day, they will try to fill the void left by their inability to exercise their passions. The sooner you are able to discover and apply your passion, the more fulfilled and happier you will become.

*Lighting the Fire*

During my freshman year at Albany State University, my class was told to meet in the auditorium. As someone who was new to college life, I was very curious about what would take place that day. We were told that we would have a speaker address the class, and that we would have to take notes about what he said, so I got my pen and paper ready. I always found motivational speakers fascinating because they thrived at something that I was completely terrified of - public speaking.

I had been known as a funny but shy child most of my life. There was something about speaking in front of a large group that made my knees shake and my voice tremble. I can remember my classmates making fun of me after having to speak in front of the class, so I always looked up to people who could do it with ease. The people who could command the attention of an audience were like superheroes to me because they were doing something that most people only wished they were able to do.

I will never forget the man who spoke to my class that day. His name was Marvin Williams, and he changed my life forever. I remember the tan suit that he wore and the confidence with which he addressed the audience. I also remember the way he moved throughout the crowd instead of standing still behind a podium. I was especially drawn to the fact that he was so much younger than any other speaker that I had heard. He made speaking seem cool. As he walked back and forth, I noticed his distinct hand motions and the inflection in his voice. A fire of excitement burned inside of me as I studied his every move. At that moment I knew I wanted to become a professional speaker. I wanted to be able to touch the lives of people all over the world through the power of words. I knew the impact that hearing motivational speeches had on me, and I wanted to deliver that excitement and entertainment as I moved through the crowd. As a country boy from a very small town, I looked to Marvin Williams and other speakers like him to help me to believe that anything was possible. Now I speak to high schools, colleges and organizations across the country as a result of the passion that was ignited inside of me that day.

*Passion is Service*

Your story may be similar to mine. Was there a great person who pointed you in the right direction or exposed you to something that changed your life? In my case, I found a way to help other people get what they wanted while helping myself live an exciting and joy-filled life. True happiness is directly related to our ability to serve those in need.

The fastest way to discover your passions is to look for ways to serve others. Our passions in life are always connected to our service to mankind. Some of us serve people directly, while others serve indirectly; yet both are equally important. For example, a person who starts a non-profit organization that provides food for homeless families is able to serve people directly. On the other hand, a sculptor who creates unique pieces of art serves others by providing them the enjoyment of admiring the work. Both of these people are servants. They just reach others differently.

*Passion vs. Money*

There are times in our lives when our passions get into a head-on collision with our desire to make money. I can remember being a high school senior and sitting down with my guidance counselor to choose my college major. I told her that I wanted to have my own business, so she suggested that I major in a specific field within business because it would be better for me when I graduated from college. I went off to do some research on the field. I wanted to know which one made the most money. After checking out some websites with salary information, I settled on marketing as a major because the average annual salary was around $60,000 and went up to over $100,000. I was sold on that major even though I didn't have a full understanding of what marketing was! Luckily, I really enjoyed marketing and business and now have several businesses of my own. Unfortunately, most people that I graduated with weren't so lucky. Many of them have never worked in the field that they studied, and some have even gone back to college to get a completely different degree. They learned just as I did that money can never be the only factor in deciding what to do with your career and life. Sure, money is important but it is a horrible indicator of what will truly bring us happiness. Most often, I find that people who go after their passions wholeheartedly are able to be compensated handsomely for what they do as well.

Those who have no idea where to start can ask themselves a few questions to get them closer to discovering what their true passions are.

*Questions to Ask Yourself*

What do I enjoy doing?

_____
_____
_____
_____

What am I good at doing?

_____
_____
_____
_____

What do others say I am good at?

_____
_____
_____
_____

What can you do for hours without noticing time has passed?

_____
_____
_____
_____

What are you willing to do for free?

_____
_____
_____
_____

What makes you angry?

_____
_____
_____
_____

What unique experiences have you gone through?

_____
_____
_____
_____
_____

How can you help others who have gone through
similar experiences?

_____
_____
_____
_____

What things can you do now that will help those in
need?

_____
_____
_____
_____

Use the questions above to provoke thought. Your answers should be able to point you in the right direction and place your feet firmly on the path toward your life's passions. It is also important to remember that as we mature the answers to these questions will change. The answers you have when you are 18 years old may be drastically different from the answers you get when you are 25 or 35 years old. Keep an open mind because your experiences will change your outlook on life. Just know that this change in perspective is a normal part of living a productive life.

## Chapter Reflections

1. Is money or happiness more important to you? Why?

   _____

   _____

   _____

   _____

2. Write down some ways that you enjoy serving others.

   _____

   _____

   _____

   _____

3. List three service organizations that you can get involved in this year.

   _____

   _____

   _____

   _____

   _____

## About The Author

Randy D. Williams, also known as "The Generation Changer," is a modern-day renaissance man. His passion for knowledge, service and motivation was shaped by his own experience. Williams tapped into his sense of purpose after losing two brothers, both under the age of 25. These events ignited his desire to effectively utilize the time that he has on Earth and to make the greatest impact possible.

As the author of several books, including Understanding and Connecting with Youth, The Young Leader's Survival Guide Series ® and 7 Questions Every Young Leader Must Answer, Randy knows how empowering it is to read. That's why he founded the Urban Reader's Association (www.UrbanReading.org) to promote and encourage reading. Furthermore, he founded Project 1322 (www.Project1322.org), an organization to mentor and teach youth about entrepreneurship in order to empower their communities.

Randy is on a mission to create the next generation of leaders and frequently speaks to college, corporate and high school audiences all over the country. He also continues to invest in several businesses through his company, Ovation Holdings, Ltd. He is based out of Hampton Roads, VA.

_____

# Connect with Randy

## Official Website

www.TheGenerationChanger.com

## Social Media

Twitter.com/ceorandy

Facebook.com/ceorandy

Instagram.com/ceorandy

Tumblr.com/ceorandy

## Email

randy@TheGenerationChanger.com